WORLD STUDIES

NORTH AMERICA

by Martha London

FOCUS
READERS.

VOYAGER

www.focusreaders.com

Focus Readers is distributed by North Star Editions:
sales@northstareditions.com | 888-417-0195

Produced for Focus Readers by Red Line Editorial.

Content Consultant: Megan C. Kassabaum, PhD, Assistant Professor of Anthropology, University of Pennsylvania

Photographs ©: iStockphoto, cover, 1, 24, 28–29; Shutterstock Images, 4–5, 7, 8–9, 11, 14–15, 17, 19, 20–21, 23, 27, 31, 34–35, 37, 38; The History Collection/Alamy, 13; Mel Evans/AP Images, 33; Agencia EL Universal/EELG/GDA/AP Images, 40–41; Darling Archive/Alamy, 43; Peter Cox/Minnesota Public Radio/AP Images, 44

Library of Congress Cataloging-in-Publication Data
Names: London, Martha, author.
Title: North America / by Martha London.
Description: Lake Elmo, MN : Focus Readers, [2021] | Series: World studies |
    Includes index. | Audience: Grades 7-9
Identifiers: LCCN 2020003742 (print) | LCCN 2020003743 (ebook) | ISBN
    9781644934012 (hardcover) | ISBN 9781644934777 (paperback) | ISBN
    9781644936290 (pdf) | ISBN 9781644935538 (ebook)
Subjects: LCSH: North America--Juvenile literature.
Classification: LCC E38.5 .L66 2021 (print) | LCC E38.5 (ebook) | DDC
    970--dc23
LC record available at https://lccn.loc.gov/2020003742
LC ebook record available at https://lccn.loc.gov/2020003743

Printed in the United States of America
Mankato, MN
012021

ABOUT THE AUTHOR

Martha London writes books for young readers. When she isn't writing, you can find her hiking in the woods.

TABLE OF CONTENTS

CHAPTER 1

WELCOME TO NORTH AMERICA

north America stretches from a thin curve of land near the equator to a vast area in the Arctic. Oceans, seas, bays, and gulfs surround the continent. Tens of thousands of islands dot those waters. Canada, the United States, Mexico, and Central America form the continent's main landmass. Central America has seven countries, including Guatemala and Panama. Canada makes up most of the continent's north. However,

Newfoundland is a large island in the Atlantic Ocean. It is part of Canada.

Greenland is North America's northernmost territory. It is also the largest island on Earth.

Much of the United States is in the middle of North America. Alaska is farther north. It lies west of Canada. The United States has the world's third-largest population. New York City is the largest US city. It is a major economic and cultural center.

Mexico lies to the south of the United States. Mexico City is the largest North American city. It is a modern urban center. But the city is also one of the oldest cities in North America. The area was home to the capital of the Aztec Empire.

Many island nations and territories are east of Mexico. This area is known as the Caribbean. Some Caribbean nations and territories include Haiti, the Dominican Republic, Cuba, Jamaica, and Puerto Rico.

Santo Domingo is one of the Caribbean's largest cities. It is the capital of the Dominican Republic. European colonizers founded the city in 1496. It remains a bustling shipping port. The city is one of many diverse places in North America.

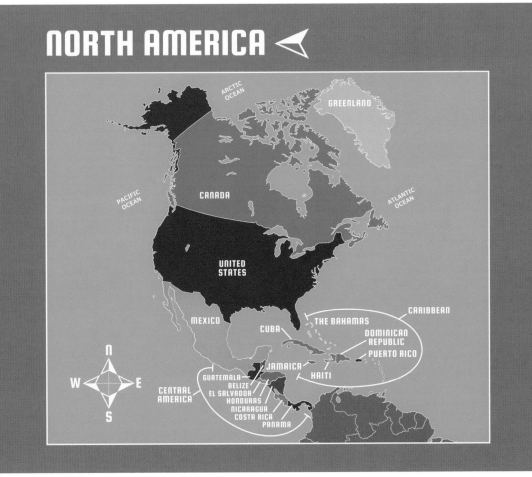

CHAPTER 2

HISTORY OF NORTH AMERICA

Humans first came to North America as early as 24,000 years ago. The continent's earliest people moved often in search of food. They spread across North America. At least 8,000 years ago, some groups started farming and settled in some areas. Others kept hunting and gathering. By 4000 BCE, groups were living in the Caribbean. By 1800 BCE, the Inuit had spread throughout Alaska and northern Canada.

The Inuit have built stone landmarks called inukshuks across Canada, Greenland, and Alaska.

Over time, many groups became more complex. In the southwestern United States, the Basketmaker culture was growing by the 1000s BCE. These peoples were skilled weavers. This culture developed into the Ancestral Pueblo culture. For hundreds of years, the Ancestral Pueblo were incredible builders.

The eastern half of the United States was also home to many cultures. In approximately 200 BCE, the Hopewell culture formed in the Midwest. These peoples were skilled copper workers. The Mississippian culture was vibrant by the 1000s CE. These peoples built massive, complex mounds out of the earth.

Other cultures formed in Mexico and Central America. By 900 BCE, the Olmec culture had developed one of the first writing systems in the Americas. By 250 CE, the Maya were building

▲ The mounds from the Mississippian city of Cahokia still stand in present-day Illinois.

huge temples. These peoples lived in dozens of cities in southern Mexico, Belize, and Guatemala. They made advances in math and astronomy.

In the early 1500s, the Aztec Empire ruled at least five million people. However, European colonizers had reached the continent in 1492. And in 1521, the Spanish defeated the Aztecs. They took over Cuba, Mexico, and Central America. In the 1600s, the French set up colonies in Canada and the Caribbean. The English set up colonies in the eastern United States and the Caribbean.

European colonization was a disaster for **Indigenous** peoples. The colonizers enslaved millions and killed many others. Europeans also brought diseases with them. These diseases were new to Indigenous people. Up to 90 percent of the Indigenous population died.

Europeans wanted new workers for their colonies. So, they enslaved millions of African people. They took Africans to North America, mostly to the Caribbean. Many also went to mainland British colonies in what is now the United States. Slaveholders used violence to force enslaved people to work under brutal conditions.

European control weakened in the late 1700s. Between 1783 and 1840, Mexico, Haiti, the United States, and most Central American countries became independent. Throughout the 1800s, US forces took over Indigenous and Mexican lands

In 1804, Haiti won independence from France. It became the first country founded by formerly enslaved people.

to the west. In the 1860s, the United States also fought a civil war that ended slavery there.

Canada united in 1867. Like the United States, Canada took over territory from Indigenous peoples. During the 1900s, Canada became fully independent. The United States became a world power. The country began using its political, economic, and military influence in Central America and throughout the world.

CHAPTER 3

GEOGRAPHY AND CLIMATE

North America is the third-largest continent on Earth. The Pacific Ocean lies to its west. The Atlantic Ocean is east. To the north lies the Arctic Ocean. The Gulf of Mexico and Caribbean Sea are southeast. North America also contains smaller bodies of water. The Rio Grande, for example, flows along the US-Mexico border. The Mississippi and Missouri Rivers flow south through the United States. They are the continent's longest rivers.

Niagara Falls is a group of huge waterfalls on the border of the United States and Canada.

Several mountain ranges also run through North America. The Rocky Mountains stretch from New Mexico to Alberta, Canada. The Sierra Madre Mountains stretch through much of Mexico.

The continent features many climates, too. For example, Alaska, northern Canada, and Greenland all have Arctic tundra. Temperatures can drop to −94 degrees Fahrenheit (−70°C). In contrast, deserts make up much of western Mexico and the southwestern United States. These areas are hot and dry. Eastern Mexico and the southeastern United States have subtropical climates. Southern Mexico, Central America, and the Caribbean are tropical. These areas are humid and rainy.

However, **climate change** is affecting all regions of North America. Dry climates have a higher risk of wildfires. Sea ice in the warming Arctic is melting. Hurricanes are stronger than in previous decades. Storms affect islands in the Caribbean and areas near the Gulf of Mexico. As climate change becomes worse, many plants and animals may struggle to survive.

CLIMATES OF NORTH AMERICA

TROPICAL
SUBTROPICAL
TEMPERATE
HIGHLAND
POLAR

N
W E
S

THE GREAT LAKES

The Great Lakes are the largest area of fresh water on Earth. This lake system covers more than 94,000 square miles (243,000 sq km). Five lakes make up this body of water. They are Lakes Superior, Michigan, Huron, Erie, and Ontario. Four of these lakes form a natural border between Canada and the United States.

Lake Superior is the deepest of the Great Lakes. Water flows from Lake Superior into Lake Huron. Lake Michigan's water also flows into Lake Huron. Then Lake Huron flows into Lake Erie, which goes into Lake Ontario. That water flows into the Saint Lawrence River. The river runs east and ends up in the Atlantic Ocean.

Indigenous peoples have depended on the Great Lakes for thousands of years. Today, the lakes provide drinking water to 40 million people.

▲ A lighthouse stands on Ontario's Bruce Peninsula, which sticks out into Lake Huron.

Many cities, such as Chicago and Toronto, line the lakes' coasts.

However, human actions are damaging the health of the Great Lakes. Some major threats include invasive species, pollution, and climate change. These threats are making it harder for plants and animals to survive.

CHAPTER 4

PLANTS AND ANIMALS

Many kinds of plants and animals live throughout North America. These life-forms vary based on climate. For instance, saguaro cacti are common in the Sonoran Desert. This desert is located in northwestern Mexico and the southwestern United States. A saguaro has a waxy coating on its skin. The coating keeps water inside the cactus. The saguaro also has sharp spines. These spines keep animals from eating the cactus.

A saguaro cactus can live for more than 150 years.

Gopher snakes can be found among the saguaros. These snakes tend to hunt rodents. They are mainly active during the day. But in the summer, gopher snakes can become active at night. That way, they avoid the hot sun.

Like North America's deserts, the Caribbean is warm. Unlike the deserts, this area receives large amounts of rain. Tropical rainforests cover many Caribbean islands. As a result, the islands contain immense **biodiversity**. Approximately 8,000 plant species can be found only in the Caribbean.

Central America also holds incredible biodiversity. For instance, Costa Rica is home to more than 13,000 species, such as the mangrove hummingbird. This bird lives only in swampy areas along Costa Rica's Pacific coast.

Farther north, the climate is cooler. But this part of the continent still gets plenty of rain.

The mangrove hummingbird is one of approximately 50 kinds of hummingbird that can be found in Costa Rica.

Forests cover many areas. Redwood trees can be found in parts of California and Oregon. They are the tallest trees on Earth.

North America's temperate climates feature plains, too. Many animal species live on the plains.

▲ American bison are the heaviest land animals in North America.

One species is the American bison. These animals mainly live in northwestern Canada and Alaska. Bison herds migrate to survive the climate. They travel south during the winter. Then they move back north when the weather is warmer.

In mountain environments, few leafy trees can grow. Pine trees such as the lodgepole survive better in these areas. This tree's pine needles handle the cold better than leaves. Lodgepoles can be found in the Rocky Mountains. They grow tall and have straight trunks.

The Rocky Mountains are also home to bighorn sheep. These animals' split hooves help them balance on the region's rocky landscape. As a result, bighorn sheep can climb steep rock faces.

Living conditions are even harsher in North America's Arctic. Few trees grow at all in the tundra. Plants and animals must survive in cold temperatures and high winds. For this reason, plants such as cotton grass grow low to the ground.

THINK ABOUT IT ◄

What plants and animals live in your area? How might they have adapted to survive in that area's climate?

NORTHERN MOCKINGBIRDS

Northern mockingbirds live in Mexico, the United States, the Caribbean, and southern parts of Canada. These birds often live in areas where temperatures are warm throughout the year. Many do not migrate. They stay in places where there is enough food and shelter all year long.

Northern mockingbirds often make their homes in open spaces or at the edges of forests. They can also be found in towns and urban areas. In the spring and summer, the birds tend to eat insects. Beetles, grasshoppers, and ants are common sources of food. In the fall and winter, the birds' diet switches to mainly berries and other fruits.

Northern mockingbirds are known for the songs they sing. These birds can learn the sounds of other animals, including humans. Northern

▲ Northern mockingbirds often build their nests high in trees.

mockingbirds learn up to 200 different songs. A mockingbird continues to learn songs its whole life. The Indigenous Nahua peoples of Mexico named this bird *centzuntli.* This name means "the bird of 400 voices."

Mockingbirds sing most in the spring and summer. They often sing to attract mates. Mockingbirds sing for long periods of time. They even sing while they build nests. However, once mockingbirds lay eggs, they do not sing in their nests. Staying quiet helps protect their eggs from predators.

CHAPTER 5

NATURAL RESOURCES AND ECONOMY

North America is home to many natural resources. For example, the continent's mountains contain a variety of metals. Iron, nickel, and lead are common in eastern mountain ranges. Western mountains tend to hold additional metals. Gold and silver are two examples.

Fossil fuels are also important to a number of economies. These fuels include coal, gas, and oil.

Open-pit mines, such as this silver mine in New Mexico, can affect huge areas of land.

The Appalachian Mountains in the United States hold vast amounts of coal. The Alberta **Basin** in Canada does as well. Gas and oil can be found in Texas and the Gulf Coast. In fact, the United States produces nearly 10 percent of the world's natural gas.

North America has a variety of other resources as well. Farther north, people cut down trees to make paper, plywood, and other products. In certain areas, farming is important. The United States is one of the largest producers of corn and soybeans. Many coastal communities also rely on fishing. Greenland depends on selling seafood to other countries for much of its economy.

However, these industries no longer form the main part of most North American economies. Manufacturing plays a larger role. For example, Canada, the United States, and Mexico produce

▲ In addition to feeding people and animals, corn is used to produce ethanol and plastics.

nearly 20 percent of the world's cars. Of the three countries, manufacturing is most important to Mexico's economy.

Some economies do not depend directly on making products. Tourism is important to Costa Rica, Belize, the Caribbean, and many other coastal areas. People visit these areas for their climate, beauty, and culture.

In addition, US and Canadian economies depend heavily on **finance** industries. Finance industries have created enormous wealth for many companies. But these industries tend not to help low-income people. Finance also tends to be risky. In fact, finance industries were the major cause of the 2008 economic crisis. This crisis caused the worst US **recession** since the Great Depression in the 1930s.

The 2008 crisis also caused problems for many other countries. The world's economies had become highly connected. The United States was also the largest economy in the world. For these reasons, the collapse of US industries greatly affected other countries.

North American economies are especially connected to one another. Mexico, Canada, the United States, and much of Central America have

⚠️ During the 2008 economic crisis, many people lost their homes because they could no longer pay for them.

been part of trade agreements for many years. These agreements lowered companies' trade costs between countries. However, they tended not to protect workers well. As a result, hundreds of thousands of jobs moved from the United States to Mexico. Wages fell across the continent as well. Mexican and Central American workers continue to receive far lower wages.

CHAPTER 6

GOVERNMENT AND POLITICS

In most North American governments, citizens select their leaders. Most of the national governments have three branches. One branch is the **legislative branch**. Citizens elect representatives to this branch directly. These representatives make laws for the country.

Members of the **executive branch** carry out the legislative branch's laws. In many North American countries, a president leads the executive branch.

A woman casts her vote during Mexico's presidential election of 2018.

He or she runs the military, too. Citizens also elect the president. Finally, the **judicial branch** decides whether laws follow the Constitution. This document describes how the government should work. It also describes certain rights that citizens have. Judges make up the members of the judicial branch. The president selects them, and the legislative branch approves them.

In Canada, Parliament makes the nation's laws. And Canada's prime minister carries out those laws like a president. But Canadian citizens do not directly elect the prime minister. Instead, they vote for lawmakers. Each member of Parliament is part of a political party. The party with the most seats in Parliament chooses a prime minister.

A variety of governments exist in the Caribbean. Some countries, such as Jamaica, have governments similar to Canada's government. In

Members of the Parliament of Canada listen to a speech by the Ukrainian president in 2014.

contrast, Cuba's government is not democratic. Between 1959 and 2018, members of one family ruled the country. The government continues to control many parts of its citizens' lives.

Throughout history, people have both supported and pushed back against their leaders. In the 1930s and 1940s, for instance, US citizens elected Franklin D. Roosevelt president four times. In 2018, Mexican citizens elected Andrés Manuel

△ Indigenous people protest the Trans Mountain pipeline in 2018. The pipeline was planned to be on Indigenous land.

López Obrador as president. He won by the most votes in the country's modern history.

In contrast, the US Congress **impeached** President Bill Clinton in 1999. He was accused of lying under oath. In 2019, Congress impeached President Donald Trump. He was accused of abusing his power to help his own political goals. In Nicaragua, people began protesting in 2018. Protesters believed President Daniel Ortega had taken too much control of the government.

In addition, Indigenous peoples across North America continue to work for the ability to govern themselves. In the United States, Indigenous nations have their own governments. They make and carry out laws on their own terms. Indigenous nations in Canada do not have their own governments. But they do hold certain Indigenous rights. However, Canadian and US governments still control these nations in certain ways. For instance, the US Congress can change what Indigenous nations have control over. Congress can even disband an Indigenous nation altogether.

THINK ABOUT IT ◁

Governments do not always serve the interests of their citizens. Can you think of an example from your own government? What could be done to make the situation better?

CHAPTER 7

PEOPLE AND CULTURE

North America has a rich variety of people and cultures. More than 1,000 Indigenous nations live throughout the continent. Approximately 15 percent of people in Mexico are Indigenous. Nahua peoples tend to live in central Mexico. They are descended from Aztec peoples. Many Nahua are skilled weavers.

In the United States, one of the largest Indigenous groups is the Navajo Nation, or Diné.

A Nahua man in central Mexico spends time with his daughter.

Some Diné artists continue traditional practices, such as weaving. Others bring Diné culture into non-native art forms. For instance, Navajo country music thrives in the Southwest.

Many people also have African ancestry. In Central America, high numbers of Black people live in Belize and Panama. More than two million Black people live in Mexico and Canada. More than 40 million live in the United States. Black Americans have contributed to all major fields. These include science, legal thought, and the arts. In fact, Black Americans helped form some of the United States' main cultural traditions.

Across North America, colonial relations still affect the lives of many people. Black people and Indigenous people often face violence and discrimination. In Canada, murder rates for Indigenous girls and women are much higher

▲ Dr. Gladys West's work as a mathematician was crucial to creating the Global Positioning System (GPS).

than for other girls and women. In the United States, Black people are much more likely to serve time in prison than white people. In Mexico, approximately 80 percent of Indigenous people live on incomes of less than $2 per day.

People with white European roots continue to have influence in other ways, too. For example, Spanish is the main language of Mexico and much of Central America. English is the most-spoken language in the United States, Belize, and Canada.

⬆ Minnesota is home to the largest Somali community in North America.

Christianity is North America's most widespread religion. At the same time, Caribbean people practice many African religions. And in Mexico, Day of the Dead celebrations combine Indigenous and Spanish-Catholic traditions.

In Canada, Métis people mix Christian and Indigenous practices. Métis have mixed European and Indigenous ancestry. Many have French and Cree roots. Some Métis speak Michif. This language blends French and Cree languages.

In addition, immigrant groups make up important parts of North American populations. For instance, more than 36 million Mexican Americans live in the United States. Millions of people also have Central American, South American, Caribbean, and Asian ancestry. In fact, the United States is home to more immigrants than any other country in the world. More than one million immigrants come to the United States every year. For reasons such as this, North America's peoples and cultures will continue to change over time.

THINK ABOUT IT ◀

What traditions does your community practice? How might those traditions combine parts of other cultures?

FOCUS ON
NORTH AMERICA

Write your answers on a separate piece of paper.

1. Write a paragraph describing the main ideas of Chapter 7.

2. North American countries exist on lands taken from Indigenous peoples. What can be done today to respond to this issue?

3. When did Canada become fully independent?
   A. the 1000s
   B. the 1500s
   C. the 1900s

4. Why might the United States have a larger Black population than Canada or Mexico?
   A. The 2008 recession caused many Black people to immigrate to the United States from Canada and Mexico.
   B. Black people are one of the Indigenous groups native to the United States.
   C. The United States enslaved many more people of African descent than Canada or Mexico.

Answer key on page 48.

GLOSSARY

basin
An area of land where smaller bodies of water drain into a larger body of water.

biodiversity
The number of different species that live in an area.

climate change
A human-caused global crisis involving long-term changes in Earth's temperature and weather patterns.

executive branch
The part of a government that carries out the laws.

finance
Business activity that uses money itself to earn more money, often involving banks, loans, credit, and investments.

impeached
Brought formal charges against someone serving in office to determine if that person was guilty of a crime.

Indigenous
Native to a region, or belonging to ancestors who lived in a region before colonists arrived.

judicial branch
The part of a government that makes decisions about legal cases.

legislative branch
The part of a government that makes laws.

recession
A time when an economy is slower, often involving less spending and more unemployment.

TO LEARN MORE

BOOKS

Harris, Duchess, and Gail Radley. *The Impact of Slavery in America*. Minneapolis: Abdo Publishing, 2020.

O'Brien, Cynthia. *Encyclopedia of American Indian History and Culture*. Washington, DC: National Geographic, 2019.

Roxburgh, Ellis. *The Aztec Empire*. New York: Cavendish Square, 2016.

NOTE TO EDUCATORS

Visit **www.focusreaders.com** to find lesson plans, activities, links, and other resources related to this title.

INDEX

Answer Key: 1. Answers will vary; **2.** Answers will vary; **3.** C; **4.** C